Wolves
{ a personal view }

by
Mark Dewolfreys

This book is dedicated to the work of the many Wolf Conservationists throughout the world who have dedicated their lives to this magnificent animal.

ISBN: 978 – 1 – 291 – 88206 – 3

Contents

All drawings and photographs are by Mark Dewolfreys

Prologue

Welcome, for those of you that have no knowledge about wolves, thank you for taking the first steps towards a better understanding of this beautiful creature and for those of you that have a little knowledge I hope that I can offer a few new facts and ideas that you did not know before.
For those of you that already know all about wolves – just look at the pictures and enjoy, and for those of you that already know all about wolves and have also got a lot of pictures – why have you bought this book ?

The following pages are of my own accounts and information that I have gathered together from various sources and then combined all the differing opinions to form a basis to produce my very own personal standard description about the wolf, I hope I have managed to explain all about the wolf, briefly, in simple layman terms. Although, if you can forgive me, in the next few pages there are a lot of scientific information for you to get through. [as well as a few Latin names thrown in for good measure]

Chapter One

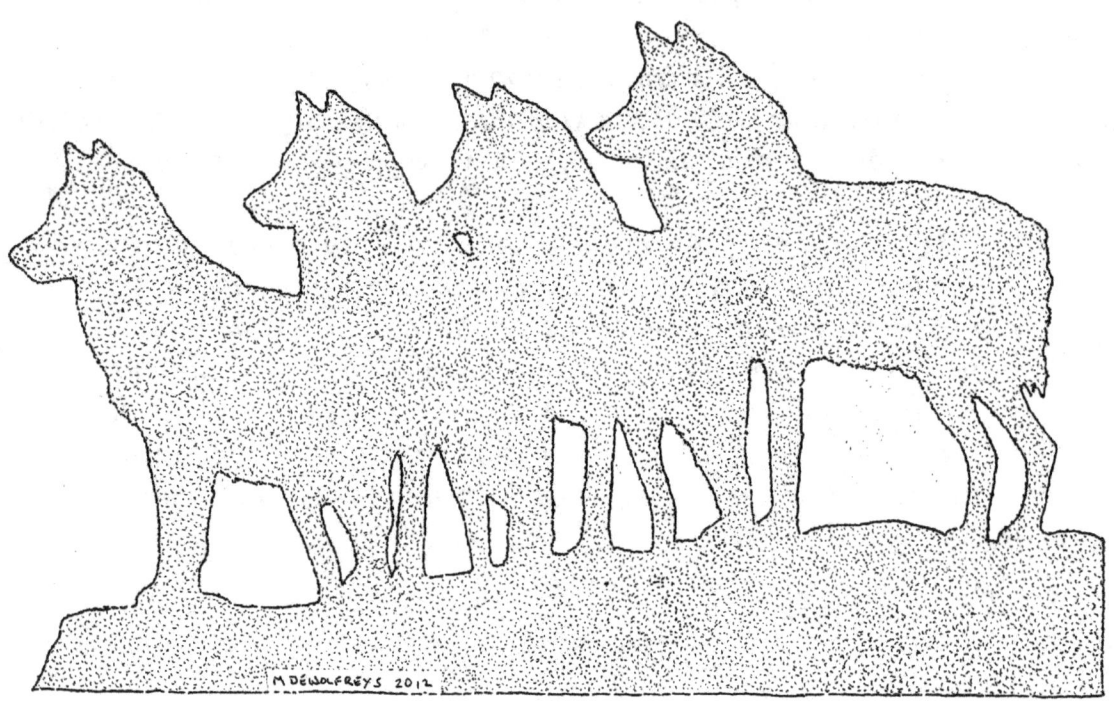

Types of wolves and their characteristics

I suppose I'd better start at the beginning – where do wolves come from?

Probably the earliest was from the primitive carnivores known as Miacids at around sixty million years ago, although there were possibly three variations of wolves that were not linked, that is to say that they were not descendent from one species.
One of these creatures known as the Dawn Wolf had a long body and a tail that looked a bit like a fox it used to climb and live in trees and was thought to be related to the feline species.
This was one of the first canidae [Cynodictis]

Don't worry I'll soon be getting through all these Latin names – I just only hope I've got all the information correct. Now where was I – oh yes

If we now speed forward forty million years to around twenty million years ago in the Miocene period Canines and Felines had branched into two separate families. The Canines or Canidae was split into several species, Wolves, Jackals, Foxes and Hyenas.

One of these animals was Tomarctus, another ancestor of the wolf it used to have a fifth toe on the hind leg, which was small and this is still evident today by the dew claw on both wolves and dogs.

Now, again, moving forward through time to about a million years ago during the early Pleistocene period the Dire Wolf [canis dirus] appeared in Eurasia, this preceded the Grey Wolf.

The appearance of the Dire Wolf was similar to the modern Grey Wolf except there were several important differences. The Dire Wolf had a larger, broader head and shorter but sturdier legs which would indicate that the Dire Wolf was probably not a very good runner. The teeth and jaws were much larger and more powerful than the Grey Wolf and it was much heavier and more powerfully built, it had Hyena like characteristics, hunting and scavenging for food, and behaved similar to the Grey Wolf by hunting in packs.

The average Dire Wolf was around five feet long, [1.5 Metres], and weighed about 125 – 175Ibs. One other difference was the brain cavity which was slightly smaller than the Grey Wolf.

Both the Dire Wolf and the Grey Wolf co-existed in North America for around four hundred thousand years along with the Coyotes, and at the end of the Pleistocene period, approximately ten thousand years ago, only the Grey Wolf and Coyote survived the Ice Age sadly the Dire Wolf became extinct.

The first specimen of a Dire Wolf was found along the Ohio River by Francis Linch in 1854

Now to the present day – there are three main species of wolf and they are –

Ethiopian Wolf *[canis simensis]* **or Abyssinian Wolf, Abyssinian Fox, Red Jackal, Simien Fox and Simien Jackal -** *which is one of the most threatened canids in the world and the only wolf species to be found in Africa.*
They are native to the Ethiopian Highlands where their current range is limited to seven isolated mountain ranges and more than half the species are in the Bale Mountains.

The Ethiopian Wolf has now become one of the world's rarest canid

It is similar in size to a Coyote and can be distinguished by its red and white fur and long and narrow skull. The thickly furred tail is white underneath and has a black tip. They have long legs and females can weigh between 11kg to 14kg [24Ibs to 31Ibs] while males can weigh between 14kg to 19kg [31Ibs to 43Ibs]
They reach their maturity at two years of age and the breeding season, which is fairly distinct, is from August to November. After a gestation period that lasts around two months, litters of two to six pups are born blind and toothless and are covered in a charcoal grey coat with a buff patch on the chest and abdomen.
The pups will emerge from their den at around three weeks, at which time their coats would have been replaced with the distinct red and white coat. By the age of five weeks they would be on a diet of milk and solid food, then by ten weeks to six months they would be completely weaned off milk.
Like the Grey wolf all the members of the pack, which can be from six wolves up to twenty wolves, take turns in looking after the pups.

The Ethiopian Wolf hunts for food on their own and only occasionally hunt together as a pack to bring down larger animals such as small antelopes. [Mountain nyala Calves or balbok]

Their main diet is rodents [Mole Rats]

The wolves live in close-knit territorial packs which consist of three to thirteen wolves and each pack can be in a area of 6km square [2 square miles] in size.

The wolves would meet up for social gatherings and territory patrols at dawn, midday and evenings whilst at night they would sleep together out in the open.

The Ethiopian Wolf has short guard hairs and a thick underfur which can withstand temperatures as low as -15 degrees. In the breeding season the female wolf's fur turns yellow and becomes woollier while the tail turns brownish and loses much of its hair. Normally the females coat is slightly paler than the males the rest of the year.

Red Wolf

Red Wolf *[canis rufus was canis lupus rufus] which can weigh up to 90Ibs, the average is 54Ibs [24.5kg] but can be from 35Ibs [16kg]*

They stand twenty-six – thirty-one inches at the shoulder. [66cm – 79cm] and during the 1980's wild Red Wolves were thought to be on the edge of extinction but since the late eighties they started to revive mainly due to captive breeding.

Red wolves have been re-introduced into north eastern North Carolina and also into the Great Smokey Mountains National Park in eastern Tennessee but these were also relocated to North Carolina in 1998

So far there are approximately 110 – 130 wolves in the Red Wolf Recovery Area in North Carolina and it is the most endangered wolf in the world.

The Red Wolf has long legs and muzzle and its coat is mostly brown and buff coloured on the upper part of body with a mixture of black, its tail is bushy with a black tip and its ears are large.

They reach maturity around two years of age and the breeding season is around January – February. After a gestation period of two months litters of three to six pups are born with slate or dark grey pelt with an auburn tinged fur on its head. Both the alpha pair look after the pups and when they are approximately six weeks old the pups leave the den.
The colour of the pelt changes to a mixture of buff, tawny, cinnamon and brown along the body then a black tip to its tail as the pups mature.

The Red Wolf lives in packs similar to those of the Grey Wolf and their diet consists of White tailed Deer, Rabbits, Rodents, Racoon, Fish and domestic livestock such as Pigs etc.

Red Wolf on the scent

Grey Wolf, [*canis lupus*] *which can weigh up to 175Ibs, the average is between 80-110Ibs and stands twenty-seven – thirty-six inches at the shoulder. The Grey Wolf has many subspecies both North American and European.*

I will briefly go over these subspecies starting with the five from the North American Wolves. They are –

Mackenzie Valley Wolves, *the largest in North America, their coats range from black to white. There are also five more subspecies within this group and they are British Columbia, Mackenzie Tundra, Interior Alaskan, Alaskan Tundra and another unknown found around Manitoba and Northern Saskatchewan.*

Artic Wolf, *which is large and stocky, their coats are white or cream in colour. There used to be two more subspecies but one of them is now extinct, [Tundra Wolf], which then leaves the Greenland Wolf.*

Buffalo Wolf, *which is now extinct, there were eleven subspecies within this group but sadly there are only five left and they are Vancouver Island, Hudson Bay, Northern Rocky Mountain, Alexander Archipelago and Baffin Island Tundra Wolves.*

In case you were wondering on the names of the extinct wolves they were the Newfoundland, Brown, Mongollon Mountain, Texas Grey, Southern Rocky Mountain and one more unknown.

Eastern / Timber Wolf, *which are grey in colour but could have black or white fur, they are found in Minnesota, Michigan and Quebec.*

Mexican Wolf, *which are the smallest wolves in North America and are usually grey in colour.*

Mexican Wolf

There are approximately eleven subspecies within the European Wolves and they are –

Arabian Wolf, *which is small with thin buff coloured fur. They are found in Southern Arabia.*

Asian Desert Wolf, *which is a small wolf found around the Black Sea.*

Common Wolf, *which is a medium sized wolf with short dense grey fur found throughout Europe and the forest areas of Russia.*

Iberian Wolf, *found in Spain and Portugal*

Steppe Wolf, *which is small with short, course, grey fur, found in the Deserts and Steppes of Central Asia.*

Tibetan Wolf, *which are medium sized wolves with long, light coloured fur, that can be found in China, Mongolia, Tibet and Southern Russia.*

Tundra Wolf, *which is a large wolf with light coloured fur, found in Northern Russia and Northern Finland.*

The next four species of wolves are unknown but come from China, Mongolia, Southern Asia between the Caspian and Black Sea and found in India near to Iraq.

Worldwide there are roughly 200,000 Grey Wolves, 500 Ethiopian Wolves and 300 Red Wolves.

Most of my own personal experiences are with Timber Wolves but I have met some European Wolves along the way. So the information I have gathered together is mostly related to the Grey Wolf species.

Grey Wolves are very similar to the German Shepherd but they have a larger head, a narrow chest, longer legs a straighter tail and bigger paws.

There are two basic types –

***The Northern Wolf** which is large in size and has a large brain and strong carnassials teeth. They inhabit North America, Europe and Northern Asia.*

***The Southern Wolf** which is small in size and has a small skull and smaller teeth. They also have short thin fur.*
They seldom howl and produce short sharp barks – they inhabit Arabian Peninsula, South Asia and North Africa
It is thought that Dogs and Dingo's stem from this group of wolves.

If you ask the ordinary person on the street what he/she thinks about wolves their first reaction would probably be one of fear, this is because they are brought up with fairy tales about the big bad wolf in stories like Little Red Riding Hood or they have seen wolves portrayed in films looking ferocious. This is far from the reality, I will go into Wolf Myths and Legends later on in this book but first let me try to explain a wolfs characteristics.

The Grey Wolf is the largest member of the dog family and, believe it or not, is the immediate ancestor of all breeds of domestic dogs from the Chihuahua to the Great Dane.

The average weight of a wolf is around 80-110Ibs and the average standing height of a wolf is from twenty-seven – thirty-two inches at the shoulder. As I mentioned earlier the largest recorded wolf weighed 175Ibs and stood thirty-six inches at the shoulder.

Wolves are very sociable animals and a wolf pack has a very complex social structure, each wolf knows its place in the wolf hierarchy.
Within the wolf family group there is a ranking system, it starts with the Alpha male and Alpha female which are supposed to be the only pair to be

allowed to mate, although this isn't always the case as there are instances where an Alpha male would mate with lower ranking females.

The Alpha pair has the choice pieces of food from the hunt, which are usually Heart, Kidney and Liver. Next would be the Beta Wolf who plays the part of protector and enforcer making sure the Alpha wolfs authority is upheld.

The Beta Wolf usually has the Rump from the hunt.

The lowest ranking wolf within the pack is the Omega Wolf and he would be left with the Stomach contents from the hunt. Their role within the pack is the most important as they act as a diffuser in tense situations, they tend to offer themselves as a sort of whipping boy.

Wolves are very intelligent creatures, resourceful and adaptable, they live in packs of about five - eleven wolves but there could be up to forty-two in a pack, but this is rare, the only time that you would find such a large pack would be in the winter time when the previous offspring would return to their old pack to join in the hunt for food.

Within the average pack you would find one to two adults, three to six juveniles and One to three yearlings.

They are carnivores and hunt Moose, Deer, Caribou, Rabbit, Hares, Badgers, Foxes, Boar, Sheep and Beaver etc. they will also eat Berries, Fruit, Apples, Pears, Melon and Nuts however, they are, along with most of the dog family, opportunists and will also hunt smaller animals including Birds, Rodents, Insects and even feed on Carrion [rotting carcases].Eggs, Lizards, Snakes, Frogs and Salmon.

They have even been known to turn to cannibalism by eating their own species.

I was lucky enough to witness a wolf capturing a stray bird that had wandered too close. The young wolf learns by trial and error as to what he can or can't eat in the way of berries etc. once again I was witness to a young wolf that had just devoured some foliage only to be sick straight away none the worse for wear, needless to say he did not try to eat that again. Wolves only eat what they require, and as they hunt to eat, any excess weight would mean that they expend more energy on the hunt. Wolves can easily starve for a week and then ingest a meal of up to 22Ibs but they often eat one day and starve the next.

A pack of wolves may travel around 50km a day but they will stay within their territory, these territories vary in size according to their source of food, therefore, where there is not much prey for the wolf, the territory would be larger like in the Artic where the territory can be over 2000 square kilometres and where there is lots of prey in abundance the territory can be as small as 100 square kilometres.

To mark the boundaries of these territories the wolves will urinate at scent marking sites, usually rocks, trees or the skeleton of a large animal. The Alpha wolves urinate by raising their legs while the rest of the pack squat to urinate. The scent marks are about every 240 metres and the smell lasts for two to three weeks

I have often thought that this could solve the problem of the wolves in Yellowstone Park that wander from their territory and start to kill livestock, as they can not fence in the wolves maybe some form of remote activated artificial scent marking along the boarders might help. I know they can use red cloth strung along but this could be impractical over a vast area.

Territorial fights between wolf packs are the principal cause of wolf mortality.

The common Grey Wolf comes in a variety of different colours it is a mixture of black, brown, red and white hairs. In the Autumn they grow their winter coat which consists of an undercoat approximately three inches thick, which will insulate the wolf from the cold.
And guard hairs approximately three and a half inches long although this could be up to five inches long.
They can withstand temperatures as low as minus 50 degrees centigrade and then in the Spring they will moult this insulating fur.

Wolves reproduce once a year, where the pups are born in the Spring in an underground den usually prepared during the summer under a tree, rock crevice or cave, but it is always near water no more than 500 metres away [1,640 feet] and with a slightly elevated view to the surrounding area. The den faces southward giving sunlight to the entrance.
They may use the same den through the generations but they also prepare several other dens for protection or any danger so they can move the pups from one location to another. They would even enlarge and use Coyote or Fox dens.
Just inside the den is a small dip to catch any rain water that might try and enter. The passageway can be anything from four foot to ten foot long which would then lead to the birthing area.
A wolf can start to reproduce when they are usually two years old, although in captivity where the food source is in abundance they can breed as young as ten months old.
The gestation period is about sixty to seventy days, only the Alpha pair can mate, again this isn't always the case.
There are usually four to six pups in a litter, each weighing approximately 1Ib. [300 – 500g]
When they are first born their overall colouring is dark brown almost black without any markings. For the first ten days of their lives they are blind, deaf and lack the sense of smell, and when a pup opens its eyes for the first time

they are usually blue / aquamarine, the colour then changes, as they get older, to orange.

In the Timber Wolf this is usually a variation of yellow / brown.

The pups can see after nine to twelve days and would start to eat solid food at about three to four weeks.

The pups rely totally on their mother for milk and warmth, at about four weeks old they would be introduced to the other members of the pack who will then help to look after them. This helps in the bonding process, the pack members would regurgitate meat for the pups

They would play fight at three weeks and this would then turn in to proper fights at five to eight weeks to establish the hierarchy and by the time they are five months old they would be large enough to travel with the rest of the pack during a hunt.

After about a year most pups are fully grown and by the time they are two years old they would have learnt to hunt successfully and the adults would then push their offspring out to form their own pack and territory.

The average lifespan of a wild wolf is between six and seven years whereas a captive wolf could live up to sixteen years or more.

A wolfs fur is made up of two layers, the outer layer is made up of long tough guard hairs which help to repel water and dirt, the inner layer is a water resistant undercoat that insulates the wolf, it is this layer that the wolf sheds in Summer.

Other characteristics of the wolf are Smell, Hearing, Sight, Taste, Teeth, Tracks and Tail, I will try to explain these as simply as possible –

Smell – The surface area receptive to smell in the wolves' nose is fourteen times stronger than that of a human. In experiments using trays of covered food, the wolf was able to detect the food within five minutes, where a dog would take over an hour to do so.
Researchers estimate that the wolves' sense of smell is up to a hundred times more sensitive than humans.
The range a wolf can detect a smell is around two to three kilometres

Hearing – Next to smell, the sense of hearing is the most powerful of the wolves' senses. A wolfs hearing ranges far beyond that of a human, they can hear up to a frequency of 26kHz, although this figure could be higher, perhaps up to 80kHz
[The highest that a human can hear is 20kHz]
It is estimated that wolves can hear as far away as six miles in the forests and up to ten miles on the open plains.

Sight – The wolves' sense of sight is quite poorly developed, most people believe that wolves are nearsighted, only seeing clearly up to seventy-five feet, but the peripheral vision and ability to detect moving objects is excellent due to the movement sensitive outer perimeter of a wolfs' retina. A wolfs' night vision is superior to a human, though they are thought to be colour blind like domestic dogs who could distinguish red from blue but not yellow from green or orange from red. Wolves can distinguish red and yellow probably because this resembles the markings like blood [red] and urine [yellow].

Taste – No one really knows what part taste plays for wolves, since smell often plays the major role in how things taste. It is known, however, that wolves have the same four taste receptors that humans have – Salty, Bitter, Sweet and Acidic.
The sweet receptor is useful to the wolves as their diet includes sweet berries and other fruits.

Teeth – The upper jaw of a wolf has six incisors which are used to cut the flesh from their prey. It also has two canine teeth, which can be up to two inches long, which are used to pierce into the flesh and hold onto the prey. There are also eight premolars and four molars which are used for slicing and grinding.
The lower jaw of the wolf has six incisors, two canine, eight premolars and six molars. The carnassials, the last premolars in the upper jaw and the first

molars in the lower jaw, are designed to slice and shear flesh. The last molars are used to grind and pulverise food prior to digestion.

A wolfs' jaw is very powerful, if you compared it to an adult Alsatian which has a jaw power of around 700Ibs per square inch, [5,200kPa], you will find that the wolf has a power of between 1500-2000Ibs per square inch, [10,340kPa], enough to snap off a human arm in one bite.

Tracks – Wolf tracks are very similar to the domestic dog, consisting of four pad prints plus claw marks. The fore print of a wolf is from four and a half to five inches in length and three and three quarters to four and a half inches in width. The rear paws are smaller in size, around three and three quarters of an inch in length and three and a quarter inches in width.

Depending on the gait of a wolf, the distance between the tracks of the hind paws and the front paws vary from twenty-five – thirty-eight inches. There is also slight webbing between each toe which allows the wolf to walk over snow or soft ground.

Tail – One significant anatomical difference to the tail of a wolf and domestic dog is the presence of a pre-caudal gland on the upper surface of a wolfs' tail, the exact function of this gland is a mystery.

The length of a wolf tail is between thirteen and twenty inches, in a male wolf the tail is between 15% - 20% larger than a female wolf. The tail can also account for approximately one quarter of the overall body length.

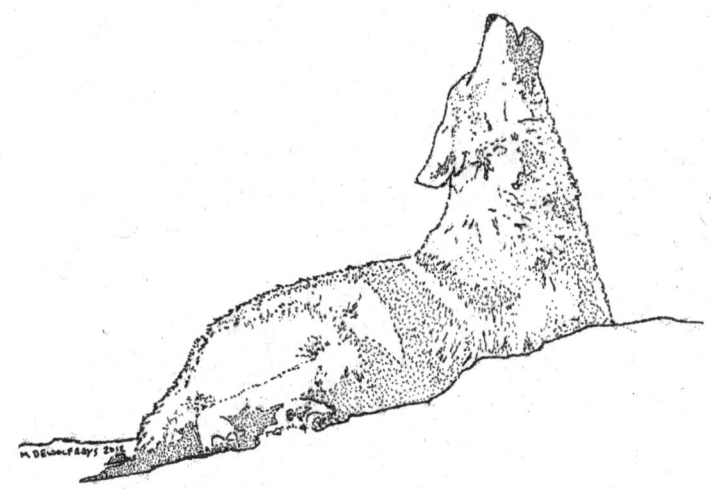

Wolves have developed a large array of signals, both vocal and postural, in order to communicate with each other. This allows the wolf to live in harmony and co-operate in the hunting and also aids in raising offspring.

Along with the body and tail positions there are also facial expressions to show just what the wolf is feeling. Here are just a few examples of postural signals –

Aggressive / Offensive Attack – *Bared teeth, tail slightly up and wagging, body low to the ground ready to pounce. Eyes open wide, staring. Ears erect and forward. Nose shortened. Hair erect.*

Apologetic / Submissive – *Ears down, tail tucked underneath, body crouching, also muzzle licking. With an intense submissive the wolf would roll on his back exposing the throat and underside, paws drawn into the body and whimpering.*

Defensive Threat – *Bared teeth and lowered head, tail down, slight crouch to body.*

Dominant – *Ears up, tail straight up, stands with an air of superiority.*

Normal – *Tail straight down.*

Running in fear – *Fear grin and ears down, tail tucked right underneath body. Head Down neck extended.*

Running in play – *Ears forward.*

When walking the wolf carries its head at the same level as its back and would only raise it when on alert. He can travel for hours at a speed of 50km/h to 60km/h [31mph to 37mph]

When he is running, the speed goes up to 55km/h to 70km/h [34mph to 43mph] this rapid burst of speed can be maintained for approximately twenty minutes although in some cases can last an hour.

The wolf can leap five metres, horizontally, in a single bound.

With vocal signals wolves not only howl but bark and whimper just like domestic dogs, by the way, wolves do not howl at the moon that is just a myth which I will go into later.
They howl for a variety of reasons but not, surprisingly, to intimidate their prey.

Here are just a few reasons why wolves howl.

When stressed, wolf pups often howl their distress.

Wolves can howl when they wake for no reason.

Wolves can howl after sessions of play or social interaction.

Wolves howl to alarm other pack members when there is an intruder.

Wolves can howl to startle prey out of hiding

Wolves can howl to attract a mate.

Wolves can howl to cement a social bond within the pack.

Wolves can howl to keep in touch with each other when separated.

Wolves can howl to announce their territory to other wolf packs.

Wolves can howl to excite and gather the pack together before a hunt.

Other vocal sounds include –

A long, smooth, howl when calling a pack to a kill

A high pitched howl when pursuing prey

A short bark and howl when closing in on prey

Harmonising howls to create the illusion of a vast pack of wolves

Barking when a wolf is startled

Growling during food challenges

Whining when wolves are curious or anxious also greeting, feeding pups or just playing

Funnily enough wolves do not respond to howls made in rainy weather

The North American Wolves initiate howling more often than their European counterparts, they say that you can feel the howl as well as hear it. When I was with some North American Wolves from the UKWolf Trust, I was privileged to be within a few feet of Kenai, who sadly died in 2006, and Kodiak, who has also sadly passed away in 2009 when they began to howl.

I had heard and read about a wolfs howl and how the sound travels great distances and that each wolf has its own unique sound, but nothing could have prepared me for what happened next.

In the top enclosure the European wolves began to howl which, in turn, set off these two older wolves. First it was Kodiak with his deep sounding howl and next to join in was Kenai, who was only a few feet away, with the most penetrating howl you could ever imagine. I could feel the howl right through my body, like a small vibrating sound wave passing right through me, it is very difficult to describe, and you really had to be there. I have heard wolves howl since that time but never have I had the same experience or feeling as I did then, I suppose I was at the right place at the right time.

The howls went on for a short while, each wolf communicating with each other then there was silence.

Many people believe that wolves howl just for the fun of it or they thought that the howl of a wolf was associated with the Devil and it was assumed that the wolf was a bloodthirsty creature that killed for pleasure.

People are still terrified of wolves because of the sound of their howling mainly due to them being misled by stories and films depicting the wolf as evil.

The wolf, when it hunts, can travel for up to an hour at speeds of 40mph which, when considering, is not very fast but to its prey it can be very tiring. Sometimes a couple of wolves would start a chase and would herd its prey into a circular pattern where other wolves, that have rested, would then take

*up the chase this would be repeated until the quarry was near exhaustion –
then the wolves would go in for the kill.*

Not all hunting expeditions would result in a kill.

Chapter 2

Wolf Myths, Legends and Facts

There have been many stories and legends that have been written about wolves over the years, here are just a few of those stories, tales and little known facts that I have gathered together.
I hope you enjoy them as much as I do –

During the Middle Ages wolves were said to have magical powers, this led to the early pharmacies to stock wolf parts such as powdered wolf liver which was used to ease child birth pain. Then there was the right paw of the wolf which, when tied around a patients throat, was thought to ease the swelling caused by a throat infection.

It was wildly believed that a horse which stepped onto a paw print, made by a wolf, would be crippled and it was also believed that a person could be blinded by the gaze from a wolf.

Another very strange belief was that some people thought that the breath from a wolf would cook meat – I know – I couldn't believe that one as well.

Dead wolves were buried at a village entrance to keep out other wolves, this is a belief by some farmers today who continue to shoot predators and hang them on fence posts to repel other predators.

The naturalists of the day believed that wolves sharpened their teeth before going on a hunt while another myth was that the early hunters and trappers use to believe that wolves were afraid of fire when, in fact, it was the men lying by the fire that kept them away.

Early travellers were warned about the perils of walking through lonely stretches of woodland and so they built stone shelters to protect them from wolf attacks.
The European term " Loup Hole or Wolf Hole ", which is a spy hole placed in the shelter so that travellers could watch out for wolves, is where the word Loophole originated.

The wolf is the only carnivore that does not defend its young, in other words self preservation is a stronger instinct than the maternal instinct, an Alpha female will simply run a hundred yards away and howl or bark at the intruder to the den. It is very rare that she would attack, she would not even try to intervene.
This just shows how deeply ingrained into the wolf is its fear of mankind.

Wolves do not make good pets but they do, however, make a much deeper bond than the domestic dog.

One of the most famous stories that were written about a wolf was Little Red Riding Hood, and what people must remember is that this is exactly what it is – a story, nothing more.
Wolves are not dangerous to humans, you stand a better chance of getting hit by a Meteorite than being killed by a wolf. Although these animals are large and powerful they do not hunt humans, there is no documented case of a healthy wolf killing a human in North America and by comparison more than twenty people are killed and around three million are attacked each year by mans best friend, the domestic dog.

In 1894 when Rudyard Kipling introduced the character of Mowgli, an Indian orphan raised by wolves, when he wrote the story The Jungle Book, there was a massive increase in wolf child stories.

Staying in the theme of India, it is reported that Child Lifting is occurring this is the phrase used when a wolf takes and kills small children, for example, in 1996 a wolf was reported to have killed dozens of small children from about fifty villages in Uttar Pradesh, Central North India.
Theories as to why this happened could be as follows –

- *There is almost no wild prey for the wolves.*

- *The wolves live very close to the human population.*

- *The wolves have lost their fear of humans.*

- *The wolves are inquisitive and they approach small, isolated children.*

- *The wolf learns that small children can be grabbed and then this spreads to other wolves or, and this is my favourite, it just might be that compensation is paid for the loss of children and in turn this might encourage some larger families, that are living in poverty, to leave their children neglected or unsupervised.*

The first comprehensive report of wild wolf attacks on humans throughout Europe, Asia and North America identified three kinds of wolf attack and these are –

Rabid – *Where wolves have gone mad because the rabies virus has infected their brain, they found that most of the fatal attacks were by rabid wolves.*

Predatory – *Unprovoked attacks where wolves appear to regard humans as their prey, but they found that there were very few fatal predatory attacks, and none recorded in North America.*

Defensive – *Where wolves are provoked by humans into attack either when they are trapped or cornered, but they found that there was no fatalities when wolves attacked defensively.*

All the attacks researched, were over a period of four hundred years and throughout the Northern Hemisphere, attacks by wolves today are very rare. Most of the fatalities were pre Twentieth Century.
Over the last fifty years researchers could only find details of approximately seventeen people killed by wolves in Europe and Russia but again none in North America. It is interesting to note that the figures correspond with the decrease of the spread of rabies in these areas.

They identified the factors for wolf attacks as being –

Rabies – *The main cause of a wolf attack.*

Habituation – *When wolves lose their fear of humans and approach too close.*

Highly Modified Environments – *This includes few natural wolf prey, human poverty and large numbers of unattended small children. This is characteristic of pre Twentieth Century Europe and India today.*

Provocation – *When humans try to molest or kill wolves*

The researchers concluded that the risk of a wolf attack in Europe and North America, today, is very low because the factors associated with wolf attacks are now rare.
Rabies does not exist in Britain and you have a far greater chance of being killed or injured by the rarity of a lightning strike.

Chapter 3

Werewolves

There are a number of cultures that have were-creatures in their mythology, usually involving large predators that hunt by night and often take the form of the most dangerous animal found in that particular area.
For example –

- *India has weretigers*

- *Africa has wereleopards*

- *Medieval Europe had the most famous, werewolves*

The term – were – is from the old English word – wer – meaning Man, therefore man-wolves or werewolves are half human and half animal. References to wolf-men came into Europe around the time of Christ, in book ten of Homers Odysseus, the grandfather of the hero, Odysseus, is named Autolykos which means – he who is wolf.

Some myths about werewolves are as follows –

The people of Arcadia believed that some members of their culture had the ability to turn themselves into wolves and if they tasted human flesh during the transformation they were doomed to live out their lives as wild beasts unless they abstained from human flesh for nine years.

People born on Christmas Eve were often thought to be werewolves

In Sicily, a child conceived during a new moon was thought to grow up to be a werewolf.

In Serbia, old folk tales told the story that people who drank water collected from a wolf paw print would turn into a werewolf.

In Greece, all epileptics were thought to be werewolves.

In Germany, an old folk tale told of a mountain brook whose water turned humans into werewolves.

The Romans believed that werewolves could not be killed as their skin was impervious to their weapons.

The Roman poet Virgil wrote, in the first century BC, about a sorcerer who took poisonous herbs to turn himself into a werewolf.

People with slanted eyebrows were automatically assumed to be werewolves.
If a werewolf suffered an injury during the night then the same injury would appear when he changed back into human form at daybreak, peasants learned to hide scars for fear of retribution as a werewolf.

Most surprisingly, even today there are those who still believe in werewolves. 80% of Russian farmers that were surveyed still believed.

One of the earliest and best known legends involving wolves is the story of Romulus and Remus, the twin sons of a Vestal Virgin – Rhea Silvia and the God Mars – who were banished to the wilderness and before they could be rescued they had been raised up by the wolves. The story originated around the fourth century BC and details how the twins went on to become the legendary founders of Ancient Rome.
Another tale about a wolf is the story by Aesop around 600 BC, it was titled The Shepherd Boy and the Wolf or as it is more popularly known as The Boy Who Cried Wolf. It was a story about a shepherd boy who has sounded many false alarms with his cry of – a wolf….a wolf – eventually they are unheeded by the townspeople, then one day, when a wolf actually arrives, to his dismay his sheep are attacked and he is left helpless.

But I seem to have digressed I should be writing about werewolves

Werewolves were originally believed to have two origins, Voluntary and Involuntary –

Voluntary Werewolves *– They were believed to be people who had made a pact with the Devil, most of the werewolf tales described men who had turned into werewolves at night where they devoured humans and animals alike after which they returned to human form at daybreak.*

Involuntary Werewolves – *They were believed to be people whose actions had inadvertently caused a horrible transformation.*

There are a lot of stories about werewolves throughout the ages but there has been no real proof of their existence. Some explanations could be that these werewolves are simply rabid wolves that have then attacked a human who, in turn, would contract the rabies disease, to the onlooker it would have looked as though he had turned into a wolf after being bitten.
Other explanations involve dreams, where a mentally unbalanced person would frequently dream that he was a wolf, then one day, became convinced that he actually was a wolf.
Some myths describe werewolf families whose curse was passed on through the generations, others tell stories about wolves raising orphaned children. The earliest accounts of wolves are probably related to its early status as a symbol of fertility.

The oldest recorded story, by Rousseau, is about a German Wolf Child from Hesse around 1344. Authorities took werewolf tales very seriously and in 1572, near the French city of Dole, the municipal government passed a law permitting out of season hunting for werewolves in order to rid their town of the terrible menace. The parliament of Franche-Comte passed a law expelling known werewolves.
The werewolf legends reached their peak, in France, in the 1600 when hundreds of innocent men and children were put to death for their imagined powers. The mentally ill or physically handicapped often paid a terrible price for their infirmities, many of them were burned at the stake.

The belief in werewolves survived in France well into the nineteenth century when peasants refused to go out at night for fear of the – loup- garou –or werewolf.

In 1685 a wolf that was preying on livestock near Eischenbach in Germany was thought to be the reincarnation of a despised town official. The wolf was killed, dressed in a suit, wig and beard and then had its muzzle cut off. A mask of the official was then placed over the face, after which it was hung.

Children who were thought to have been raised by wolves, or any wild animal, were often referred to as wolf-children simply because they behaved like wild wolves. These children hated to wear clothes, they had a liking for raw meat and sought the dark during the day and roamed about during the night.

They howled, ripped at the flesh of those that tried to care for them, curled back their lips in a snarl to indicate their displeasure, panted like a dog when they were hot and ran around on all fours.

One of these wolf-children was a wild boy from Aveyron called Victor, who exhibited most of the previous symptoms. He was treated by the French physician Jean Itard for many years and during that time Victor never learned to speak and he remained confused about his sexual desires right up until his death at the age of forty.

Another story, still in France during the seventeenth century, involved a boy of thirteen named Jean Grenier. He was partially idiotic and had a strong marked canine appearance. His jaw stuck forward and his canine teeth showed under his upper lip, he believed that he was a werewolf. One evening when he met some young girls he terrified them by saying that as soon as the sun had set he would turn into a wolf and eat them for supper. A few days later one little girl, having gone out at nightfall to tend the sheep, was attacked by some creature which she believed was a wolf. She beat the creature off with her staff then fled back home, the creature was later to be identified as Jean Grenier. When he was brought before the law courts of Bordeaux he confessed that two years earlier he had met the Devil one night and signed a pact with him, in return for this pact he received a wolfs skin. Since then he has roamed about as a wolf after dark, resuming his human form at daybreak. He claimed he had killed and eaten several children whom he had found alone in the fields, one time he had entered a house whilst the adult family were out and taken a baby from its cradle. A careful investigation by the court proved that these statements were true, certainly as far as the cannibalism was concerned.

There is no doubt that the missing children were eaten by Jean Grenier and there is no doubt that the half witted boy was convinced he was a wolf. The court displayed a depth of compassion unusual for the period, it took into account both the boys tender age and the medical opinion which was that Grenier was a victim of Delusional Insanity or Lycanthropy – **Lycanthropy is a medical illness whose victims believe they are a wolf.**

Jean Grenier was sentenced to life imprisonment within the walls of the Franciscan Monastery in Bordeaux.

The idea of a werewolf being the victim of insanity was by no means new, a few years earlier fourteen people were tried in France for sorcery and werewolf transformations and were subsequently acquitted, but Greniers case does mark the beginning of a new approach to werewolfism.

Judges were becoming more and more convinced that many suspected werewolves were, in fact, patients suffering from various forms of mental delusions, a form of madness not helped by the potent drugs and incantations with which many of these patients indulged themselves.

It is from this time that men of law and medicine started to subdivide people with animal delusions into two distinct categories –

Werewolves – *Was the mythical creature*

Lycanthropes – *Was the mental patient*

Chapter 4

Native American Indians

The American Indians referred to the wolf as – Brother – and they used the wolf as a spirit guide. Great Warriors, Medicine Men and Indian Chiefs took wolf names, and their exploits were retold around the camp fires. So powerful was the medicine of the wolf, elite warrior societies believed that by putting on the pelts of wolves and making themselves resemble the wolf before riding into the camps of their enemies, they would become invisible and virtually invincible.
The following is a list of tribes and their meaning relating to wolves –

- ***Acoma** – meaning wolf robe*

- ***Apache** – meaning wolf face*

- **Blackfoot** – *meaning wolf leg*

- **Blood** – *meaning wolf in the water*

- **Cheyenne** – *meaning little wolf*

- **Crow** – *meaning wolf goes to drink*

- **Hidatsa** – *meaning wolf eyes*

- **Kiowa** – *meaning sleeping wolf*

- **Lakota** – *meaning high wolf*

- **Nez Perce** – *meaning yellow wolf*

- **Palouse** – *meaning wolf necklace*

- **Peigan** – *meaning wolf tail*

- **Seminole** – *meaning mad wolf*

- **Stoney** – *meaning wolf teeth*

A number of Native American tribes had Medicine Men who put on wolf skins in order to duplicate their powers.

The two tribes that identified most strongly with the wolves were the Pawnee and Cheyenne, the Pawnee identified so closely with the wolf that their hand signal for the wolf was the same as the hand signal for the Pawnee.

The Cheyenne Medicine Men rubbed wolf fur onto arrows to bring them good luck whilst they were hunting and they were also the best known of all Indian Wolf Societies because of their Wolf Soldiers who were fierce fighters that were dreaded by both settlers and soldiers alike.
The Pawnee, Hidatsa and Oto Indians all had wolf bundles which were pouches made of wolf skin that guarded treasured bits of feathers and bones used in magic ceremonies.

The Sioux name for a wolf is – Shunk manitu tanka – which means – Animal that looks like a dog but is a powerful spirit.

The Nootka Indians of the Pacific Northwest had a ceremony in which the son of a Chief was pretending to be killed and then he was brought back to life by Indians wearing wolf robes and wolf head hats.
The ceremony reinforced the close spiritual ties, they believed, they had with the wolf, other Pacific Indians had similar beliefs.

The North American Indians mentally became wolves through Animist Societies.

The Arapaho Indians had a wolf division whilst the Caddo Indians had a wolf band

The Crow Indians, from Montana, had a Crow Wolf Society whose members draped themselves in wolf skins prior to hunting.

The Mandan Indians wore wolf tails on their moccasins as a badge of success in battle whilst the Assiniboine Indians wore white wolf skin caps into battle for good luck.

The Hidatsa Indian women, experiencing difficult childbirth, used to rub their stomachs with wolf skins.

The Cree Indians believed that heavenly wolves visited the Earth when the Northern Lights shone in winter, and of the hundreds of recorded wolf legends one of the best known is the Cree story of the Earth Maker Wolf and the creation of the World.

This is how the story goes –

While all the land was covered with water, the trickster, Wisagatcak, pulled up some trees and made a raft and on it he collected many animals swimming in the waters.

The Raven left the raft for a whole day but he saw no land, so Wisagatcak called the wolf to help. The wolf ran around and around the raft with a ball of moss in his mouth, the moss grew and the Earth formed on the moss, it spread on the raft and kept on growing until it made the whole World.

This is how the Earth was created.

Some tribes believed that killing a wolf would cause the big game to disappear and it was common for Indians to interpret natural history in terms of wolf behaviour.

A number of tribes thought that wolves howl after eating in order to invite scavengers to come and devoir what was left, whilst many others believed that the wolfs' howls were the cries of lost spirits trying to return to the Earth.

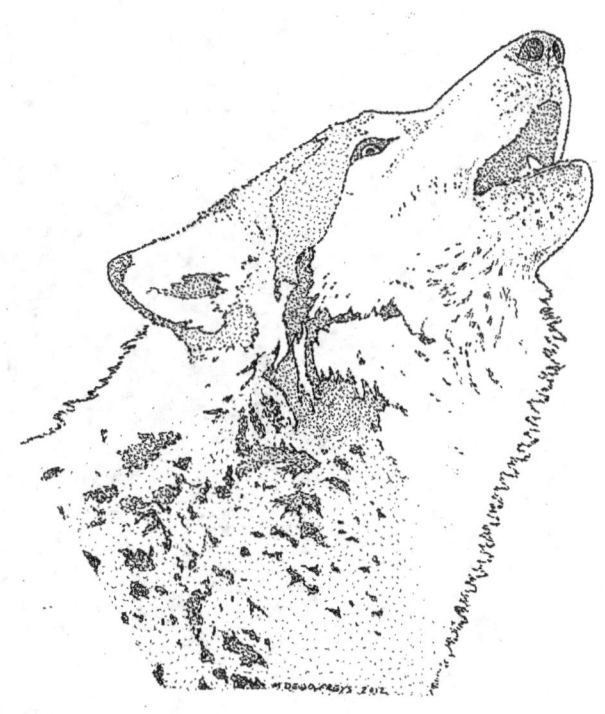

Chapter 5

Wolf History in the UK

When man was pursuing a hunter / gatherer existence, initial relationships with wolves were viewed with a mutual respect, as their common prey of Deer, Rabbit and Boar etc. were in abundance and competition for food or land space was rare. This lasted until humans switched to an economy based on farming and keeping of livestock. Gradually the landscape was converted to pastures and crop areas, for the wolf this loss of habitat brought about a subsequent reduction in prey animals with the wolves territory being drawn closer to human inhabited regions in order to exploit the available Sheep and Cattle stocks.

In Scotland the wolves demise was slower, the reason for this was attributed to the vast forests and moor land, the districts of uncultivated land and, most notably, the difficulty of communication between scattered communities, for example – the wolves were sheltered from organised persecution. However, in these early times as well as the wolf being branded the herdsman's enemy, wolf hunting amongst Kings and Nobles was considered the most exciting of all the field sports.

The records of the wolf presence in Medieval Britain are clearer with descriptions of wolf numbers mainly being confined to the Welsh border counties and in the North. In the tenth century, King Edgar of England imposed an annual tribute of three hundred wolves on the Welsh King, Lundwall. He also allowed men to pay taxes in wolf heads whilst granting amnesty to criminals bringing forth one hundred wolf tongues.
Subsequent records clearly indicate the wolfs' presence in England at least until the fourteenth century where encounters became rare during hunting. The main cause of the wolf decline was the habitat loss in the form of deforestation.

When the Romans arrived in Britain, wolves were numerous although it is not known how widespread they were in Anglo-Saxon times. During this time it was believed that wolves were at their most active, in the coldest period of the year, January, the Anglo-Saxons named this month as the Wolf Month.
The last wolf believed to have been killed south of the Scottish border was sometime in the 1480's.

In Scotland during the fifteenth century, under the rule of James I, the wolf was still perceived as a pest, reaching its peak during the reign of Queen Mary Stuart where laws were passed forcing all Scottish men to participate in wolf hunting three times a year. By the 1600's the various methods of hunting the wolf had still not exterminated the creature, so more extreme

measures were used. Although not proven, there are stories of the forests of Rannoch and Lochaber being deliberately burned in order to destroy the wolf dens and also to deny them any cover.
In the Highlands this trend was reflected in the vast Caledonian Pine Forrest which was originally 1.5 million hectares in size but by the 1600's it was down to 170,000 hectares.

The last positive record of wolf presence was in Sutherland in 1691 where the large sum of £6.13s was paid for a wolf.

The last wolf in Scotland was shot in 1743 at a place called Tomatin in the Findhorn Valley, the wolf was shot after allegedly devouring two children, however, many authors doubt the validity of this story especially as the tale was published some eighty years after the event.

The heaviest wild wolf weighed 175lbs and was killed in Alaska in 1935

Chapter 6

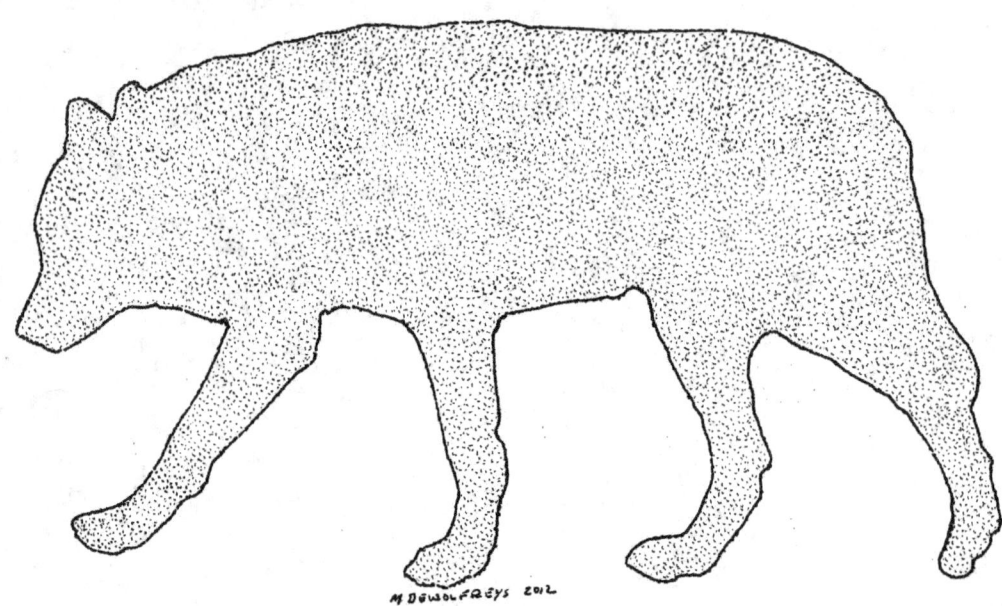

M DEWOLFREYS 2012

My own wolf experiences

Over the years I have had many close encounters with wolves and I hope to have a lot more as the years go on. I have always had a fascination with wolves, I suppose it was inevitable with a surname like mine.

Growing up I was always taunted with phrases like – it's da wolf… it's da wolf – or you get the really smart ones who tended to howl whenever I was around, and if I only had a pound every time I heard that one I'd be a millionaire by now.

Like most people from my generation I had been brought up with stories like – The Big Bad Wolf or Little Red Riding Hood – even today people still tend to fear the wolf thinking they are viscous animals that will attack anything and anybody for no reason – again this is due to Hollywood portraying their version of wolves in horror films - this instilled the wrong perception so, as I grew older, I decided to learn more about the wolf and its habits. I started by reading books by L David Mech and the more I studied the more I wanted to meet these fascinating creatures at first hand.

My first encounter with wolves was with the UKWolf Conservation Trust based in Reading, Berkshire.

They have ten wolves consisting of two packs – and two pairs

The Beenham Pack – *is made up of three siblings, Nuka a male Northwestern Wolf, also known as Mackenzie Valley Wolf or Northern Timber Wolf. [canis lupus occidentalis]*
He can be affectionate and bold but with a hint of naughtiness.
Then there is his sister Tala the black wolf of the Beenham pack, which is the lowest ranked wolf, and the last wolf in the pack is Tundra their other female sibling
All three wolves were born on the 3ʳᵈ May 2011 at the UKWolf Conservation Trust and work as ambassadors for wolf conservation.

The Arctic Pack – *is also made up of three siblings, Pukak a low ranking male Artic Wolf. [canis lupus arctos] Then there is Massak, the largest of the three Arctic wolves who can be quite shy and reserved. He is like the lookout of the pack, and then finally Sikko their sister a friendly wolf who likes to greet people she knows. She also works as an ambassador for wolf conservation where she is involved in behavioural research with students of all levels. This takes place on site.*
They were born during a snow storm on the 8ᵗʰ March 2011 at Parc Safari, Canada – they were hand reared to recovery by the team at the Parc Safari as it was feared that when they were found they were not going to live – when the pups were around ten weeks old they were sent to the UK and, at the time, were the only Arctic Wolves in Britain.

First Pair - Mosi and Torak –

Mosi *a female Northwestern Wolf who is bold, likes attention, full of energy and inquisitive. She is a very vocal wolf that speaks in a low grumble / growl Born on the 27th April 2006 at Dartmoor Wildlife Park*
Mosi means " cat " in the Navajo language
Torak *a male European / Northwestern Wolf cross [C I lupus x C I occidentalis] He was named after the Stone Age boy in Michelle Pavers book – The Chronicles of Ancient Darkness. And he is probably the largest wolf at the Trust, he can be stand – offish and a little apprehensive.*
Born on the 22nd April 2006 at the Anglian Wolf Society
Both these wolves have now been retired from the public walks as they found them too stressful.

Second Pair – Mai and Motomo –

Mai *a female Northwestern Wolf who likes being around people – a very majestic wolf but when she gets too excited she can jump around eight foot straight up in the air which could cause an injury if she fell awkwardly.*
Born on the 27th April 2006 at Dartmoor Wildlife Park
Motomo *a male Northwestern Wolf who was hand reared for the first two weeks of his life – he is one of the largest wolves at the Trust*
Born on the 19th May 2008 at Combe Martin Wildlife and Dinosaur Park

On the 3rd May 2011 Mai gave birth to four cubs – The Beenham Pack – one of the cubs was stillborn.

The former wolves that I can remember were –

Northwestern pack *– which was Duma, an Alpha female who was born on the 12th May 1998 and passed away on the 12th November 2012, her sister, Dakota who was sadly diagnosed with Lymphoma Cancer in 2007 and passed away in 2010. Previously she had lost six inches of her tail due to a dispute with Lunca one of the European wolves.*

European pack *– which was Latea, an Alpha female, born on the 3rd May 1999 and passed away on the 26th May 2011 her sister Lunca, a Beta female, who passed away on the 9th January 2013 and finally their brother, Alba who broke a vertebra in his neck back in 2005 then finally lost his fight for* *life on the 23rd January 2010 after losing the use of both hind legs. These were probably the first wolves to be successfully bred in England for around five hundred years.*

The two Northwestern wolves that I fondly remember were known as the Old Couple. Kenai, an Alpha female who passed away in 2006 due to cancer and Kodiak, an Alpha male who moved in with his younger sisters Duma and Dakota until he sadly passed away on the 11th February 2009 aged fourteen. Both these wolves were the founders of the Trust.

Roger Palmer, who had kept wolves for over thirty years, founded the UKWolf Conservation Trust back in May 1995 with the aim of using the wolves to dispel the many myths and misconceptions that surrounded these magnificent animals.
The Trust is open to the public, although you would have to arrange a time with them for when you can go to visit – they offer Photography Courses, Lectures, Study Courses and various other activities involving their wolves.
[I will go into these in depth later on]
They are involved in projects all over the world including – Armenia, Bulgaria, Croatia, Ethiopia Greece, Russia and the USA where they have projects on the Mexican and Red wolves.

One activity that the Trust does is to go walking with the wolves through Ufton Woods in Reading, this is a well organised trip which lasts around two hours. I have been on one of these treks and I would thoroughly recommend that you try this.

This is, briefly, what happens –

You'll receive instructions on what to wear, for example – Wellington Boots or Walking Boots with the laces tucked in, sensible clothing but not Suede, Leather or brightly coloured clothing and definitely no strong perfumes or aftershave. Any loose jumpers or any other loose clothing should either, not be worn or tucked in firmly out of harms way – now my wife can testify to this as she had an altercation with Tamaska, a black Timber wolf, when he was just a pup. I shall go into that tale later on.
It is not advisable to bring any bags or have any food on your person and with cameras, you need to keep these safe out of harms way or should I say – out of the wolfs' way.

You all meet at a prearranged time at one of the entrances to the woods and, once there, you'll meet up with some of the handlers who will check to see if you are dressed properly and also they will explain what to expect when the wolves arrive. Sometimes there may only be one wolf arriving to go on the walk, this just depends on the day.
Next you are all told to form a line and hold your hands out in a fist in front of your body so that the wolves can go down the line and sniff your scent. If you are lucky the wolves may stop and lick your fist and if you're really lucky they could even grasp your fist into their mouth. If this does happen, do not pull away as the wolf would treat this as a sort of game, and they would win hands down in a tug of war situation. Now to the wolf, gripping your fist in their mouths is a form of greeting, a bit like shaking hands.
After this initial intro, the wolves would be eager to carry on with the walk. You have two volunteers from the Trust in front of the wolves making sure that no members of the public suddenly appear, either with their own dogs, on foot or on horse back. There are, at least, two handlers with each wolf and a further volunteer bringing up the rear. In amongst the group are a couple more volunteers from the Trust answering questions and every now and then the handlers would stop the wolves for photo opportunities. Halfway through the walk there is a small lecture on wolves after which the walk continues with a few more stops along the way for more pictures and handling of the wolves. After they arrive at the lake the wolves are allowed to cool off then this is the cue for returning back to the starting point.
You then make your way to the Centre where you can meet the other wolves and have a well deserved cup of tea.

Their wolves have often been used in film work and their list of credits include – Company of Wolves, Dracula, American Werewolf in London and Monarch of the Glen.

As I mentioned earlier they have several Membership / Activities and they consist of –

Walking Membership – *which is as described above where you walk with the wolves for a couple of hours then return to the Centre for refreshments before seeing the rest of the packs. There are loads of photo opportunities from a raised platform and special gaps in the wolf enclosures. You will also receive a wolf photograph and a subscription to the Wolf Print Magazine.*

Childrens Wolf Walk – *Where you will walk with the wolves around the fields at the trust and you will be able to take photographs from a raised platform. There is also a tour of the Trust to see the other wolves.*

Wolf Viewing and Bat Walk – *where you go to the Centre to see the different packs of wolves and are able to take photographs from a raised platform. You will also have the opportunity of a howling session and seeing the wolves feed. Next there is a talk on Bats followed by a walk around the Trust at dusk to see long-eared bats flying above you whilst you hear the bats ultrasonic calls.*

Howl Nights – *where you come along and try to get the wolves to interact with you howling [There is no contact with wolves or any walks with wolves on this event]*

Arctic Amble – *where you walk with the Arctic wolves*

Wolf Keeper Experience – Wolf Keeper Day – *where you will shadow a keeper behind the scenes at the Trust and help in cleaning the wolf enclosures and preparing their food. You will also be involved in the Wolf Enrichment Programme where food is hidden in various places around the enclosures and also in various objects such as Hessian sacks or cardboard boxes to help stimulate the wolves in finding food.*
You will also spend some time monitoring their behaviour and after lunch you will have the opportunity to go on a wolf walk.
Throughout the day you will have plenty of photographic opportunities and at the end of the day you will receive a souvenir Certificate.

Adopt a Wolf – *where you will receive a photograph of your chosen wolf plus a Certificate, three Wolf Print Magazines and a bottle of real Wolf Hair from your adopted wolf.*

There are also Photography Days, Predator Flying Experience / Wolf Talk and Work Experience for College / University Students who are interested in Conservation and Animal related projects. This latter Course is for a minimum of two weeks and covers all aspects of Wolf and Centre Management.
Their web site offers a great deal of information and is updated regularly – I bet now that I've put that, the web site will stop working and close down.
I should mention here that all the web site addresses and other such information has been listed at the end of my book and they were correct at the time of press – there that's the legal jargon out the way – now to continue.

It was from one of the volunteers at UKWolf that told me about Shaun Ellis and his work with wolves, he recommended that I read his book entitled – The Wolf Talk – it is about Shaun's early life with wolves.
After reading his book we decided to go to Combe Martin in Devon where Shaun used to run Wolfpack Management.

They had sixteen wolves consisting of two packs and they were –

***European –** which were Norook, Zarnesti and Totto all three were male wolves.*

***Timber –** which was made up of four generations of Timber Wolves, the first or oldest generation was Elu an Alpha female and Pale Face an Alpha Male. This was followed by the second generation born in 2004 from a liaison between Elu and Pale Face, they were Yana the Alpha male whose name means Bear, Tamaska the enforcer or Beta male whose name means Mighty and Kind and lastly Matsi another male wolf whose name means*

Sweet and Brave. There was a fourth black pup named Cheyenne but she sadly died.

The third generation, born in 2006, were from a liaison between Elu and Shadow, who sadly died, and they were Cheyenne a female wolf whose name means Little Wolf, Nanoose a male wolf whose name means Push Forward, Nataa another male whose name means The Speaker and then, finally Tejas another male whose name means Friend to all.

The fourth and last generation born in 2008, were from a liaison between Cheyenne and Yana, and they were Ayet a female wolf whose name means Little Sister, Amick a male whose name means Little Talking Brother, Lapwai who was the smallest male whose name means He Me and last of all Motomo another male whose name means He who goes first.

I suppose we had been lucky really, as our first close encounter was to see Tamaska, Matsi and Yana when they were only six months old. These were the pups that Shaun Ellis was living with for about a year, and raising them up as a wolf would because Elu was not looking after them properly.

It was after the lecture, at the main wolf enclosure, had finished that Alan, one of the handlers, asked if we wanted to see the wolf pups. There were about six of us in the group and we were advised on what to expect when we see the pups, we were taken down a narrow pathway alongside the enclosure of the European Wolves. We were all told not to get too close to these wolves as they were wild and they would treat us as invaders to their territory. One of the group, did, however, get a little too close and before he knew it one of the European wolves pounced, he had been silently stalking him. Luckily the fencing saved him.

We were all led into a small enclosure, the size of a small canine enclosure, approximately ten foot by twelve foot. Alan explained that we all needed to lean against the fencing so that when the pups arrived into the enclosure they wouldn't knock us down – by then I was slightly worried. Alan explained that we must not lean over the pups as they may jump up, and as they are no good at judging distances, this could result in a broken nose – which Alan delighted in telling us had already happened to him three times since the wolves were born. – Ok so now I was getting more worried.

The reality of the situation sunk in when Alan told us that we should put away any cameras, tuck in any loose clothing or anything else that the pups could get hold of, as they cannot be held responsible for the action of the pups. There we were standing along the fencing with our hands held in a fist in front of our bodies waiting for the arrival of the pups. Alan suggested that we might like to kneel down, if we wished, and if the pups get too boisterous we could always stand up again and they would leave us alone, well that was the theory anyway. As predicted none of us knelt down and it was at this point that Alan opened the door to the pups inner sanctum and we all waited with anticipation of the pups arrival – but nothing happened – no pups, no movement not even a stir.

The pups were still eating – it was one of those moments when you've got yourself all psyched up and then you're let down with a bang then just as we all started to relax out came this huge black Timber Wolf called Tamaska, this would be my first, of many, meetings with this particular wolf.

He went down the line of people sniffing their fists until he reached me, now I don't know what I did to deserve what happened next but I will certainly never forget it.

There I was standing against the fence, all five foot six of me, when Tamaska decided that instead of sniffing my fist, like all the others, he wanted to lick and muzzle my face all over. This six month old pup the size of a fully grown Alsatian had no trouble reaching my face, this went on for what seemed an eternity but was, in fact, probably only a minute.

After Tamaska had finished along came Yana a more sedate pup which was more cautious and, surprisingly, smaller than Tamaska.

By now I was kneeling down mesmerised by their presence and it wasn't long before Tamaska came back for more licks.

It was following this episode that Tamaska then turned his attention to my wife, Meryl, she was standing by the fence when he decided that her scarf, which had been tucked in out of harms way or so she thought, was going to be his scarf. Now a tug of war had begun, not that this was going to be much of a war with a huge powerful wolf tugging at her scarf, luckily for my wife Alan came to the rescue and the scarf was saved – and so was my wife.

On this occasion we never did get to see the third wolf pup, Matsi, too busy eating I suppose, but we were lucky the next time we went, not only did we see Shaun we also watched his lecture and saw the elusive Matsi.
For those of you who were wondering why I didn't go to the rescue it was because I wanted to leave it up to the experts – well that's my story and I'm sticking to it.

We returned in March 2005 to see how all the pups were getting on – my how they had grown.
They were nearly a year old and we were treated to Shaun conducting the Wolf Talk at the main enclosure.

Three months on we returned to see Tamaska and Shaun in the top field by the European Wolf enclosure and by now Tamaska was huge, apparently he had not stopped growing.
He was still his usual playful self, very inquisitive, and he loves all this attention. That's Tamaska not Shaun in case you're wondering.

Then the next time we came to visit was in April 2007 to see Tamaska and the new pups – Cheyenne, Nataa, Tejas and Nanoose – who were then a year old.

Shaun had also come in on his day off – we would like to think that this was especially for our benefit, but I don't think he could tear himself away from the wolves. He presented us with signed copies of his new book – Spirit of the Wolf – which he did in collaboration with Monty Sloan who had supplied the photographs.

Tejas looks just like Tamaska did when he was a pup, whilst Cheyenne, Nataa and Nanoose look like Matsi. Yana, being the Alpha Male, is slightly darker in colour.

We met with Linda and Roger, two new handlers, who took us down to the new revamped enclosure and inside were Cheyenne and Nataa. During their lecture, Cheyenne, being more inquisitive than Nataa, came close to the fence line whilst Nataa, unfortunately, seemed more interested in uprooting a tree that had been recently planted in the enclosure. It was in minutes that he had dug a huge hole and now the tree was listing at an angle of forty-five degrees.

After the lecture we were told to hang around until all the others had gone and they would try and see if we can go into the enclosure to see the pups. We were told that Tamaska had taken on the role of looking after the new pups and he would have to vet anyone going in to see them first – if he disapproved then we wouldn't be allowed in.

We were not worried as we knew Tamaska well – and when he saw us he came bounding over to the fence line and, to the astonishment of the new handlers, he rolled straight onto his back waiting for some affection.

This was just like the old Tamaska we knew and loved.

With approval given we entered the main enclosure and waited up against the fence, Cheyenne wasted no time at all to investigate the new intruders in her domain, the first thing she did was to jump up and lick my wife's face then she turned her attention to me.

Now Cheyenne didn't just stop at licking my face – oh no – she kept on rubbing herself against my legs then rolling about on her back chewing at my shoes, much to the delight of the handlers and my wife who thought I must have something hidden in my shoes.

Cheyenne then started gripping my calf and then went onto my hand – it is a strange feeling, there is just enough pressure to feel slightly uncomfortable but not enough to penetrate the skin.

It's like she is testing to see how far she can go.

After about fifteen minutes, or what seemed longer, Cheyenne gave up and started to walk about the enclosure whilst all this time Nataa had kept his distance.

Tamaska came over to the fence line to see what he was missing out on so Meryl started making a fuss over him through the fence. All this new attention brought Nataa over but no sooner had he arrived when Cheyenne decided she wanted to play, rather roughly, right in front of us. Nataa tried to hide between my legs and the fence line but Cheyenne was having none of that and promptly dived in to drive Nataa away.

I made my way to the small waiting area, this is an area approximately four feet square with a gate into the enclosure and a gate leading out, unfortunately Nataa had the same idea and we both ended up trapped in this small place with Cheyenne at the entrance also trying to get in. As luck would have it Nataa stood on a Mattock and this, in turn, made him jump and run out of the waiting area hotly pursued by Cheyenne.

By the time we had left the main enclosure the rest of the pack had come down the hill to find out what had been going on, they were all excitedly huddled together, sniffing and rubbing as wolves do when they return from trips – they use this method of scent tracing to find out.

It was at this point that I realised I had not taken any pictures as I was so engrossed in watching the wolves interact with one another, luckily for me others had taken some. We headed back to the centre to take another look around, Shaun was still there answering questions and explaining his life with wolves. We, however, were covered in mud courtesy of Cheyenne and

Nataa and as we walked around the room Shaun said – I can see you two have had a good time.

We returned in October, that same year, to see the newly formed wolf pack which now consisted of seven Timber Wolves made up from Yana the Alpha Male, Tamaska the Beta male, Matsi, Cheyenne, Nataa, Nanoose and Tejas.

It would be another year before we returned to the Centre, they had four more new pups that were six months old and they were Ayet, Amick, Motomo and Lapwai.
It was raining the day we came and Nataa and Tejas had been separated from the rest of the pack as they were now of an age to question the leadership, they had been placed in an adjoining enclosure while all the rest of the pack were in the main enclosure.

Sadly Tamaska had hurt his paw so he was keeping out of the way so as to not show any injury to the rest of the pack as this might be seen as a weakness in his authority.

Linda called to see if any of the wolves would come over to the fence line to see us but, as they had all just eaten, all they wanted to do was relax and sleep.

Nataa and Tejas on the other hand were far more curious to our presence and came running over when we were close to their enclosure. We placed our hands against the fence and they both started sniffing then rubbing their bodies against us, this is just another way of sending a message back to the other members of the pack, by using their scent, as they knew we would eventually return to the main enclosure.

We managed to get some very good pictures once the wolves had settled down, despite the rain, and it wasn't long before we had to leave them in peace.

But before we finally left we did try to see Tamaska in the main enclosure but he was having none of it.

Maybe next time.

It was in March 2009 when we returned to see how Tamaska was fairing with his paw, Nataa and Tejas were still separated from the rest of the pack along with Cheyenne. The weather was much better and we managed to get some great pictures of the packs, even Tamaska was fairing well.

We brought along our friend Vicky, who is studying at Newquay Zoo College, she wanted to learn more about the wolves and their habits. Unfortunately there was no Wolf Talk happening that particular day and they had also lost the use of their Wolf Centre but Vicky did manage to learn quite a bit thanks to Roger, one of the handlers, and she also managed to get up close and personal with the wolves.

Lots of people started to gather round when we were with the wolves wondering what was going on, and with all this attention Tamaska and Matsi were getting slightly agitated and started to pace along the fence line in their enclosure.

In the other enclosure Nataa, Tejas and Cheyenne were quite happy just to pose for pictures and they appeared not to be put off by all the attention.

It was after the photo session that we were told of the sad news that Shadow had died of a heart condition a few weeks previous to our visit that day, he shall be missed greatly. Pale Face and Elu were coping well with the loss of their companion.

Wolfpack Management used to be based at Combe Martin Wildlife and Dinosaur Park in Devon, then they moved to the other side of Combe Martin to Newberry Farm, Woodlands and called themselves The Wolf Centre. They have now moved again and have temporary accommodation at Dartmoor Zoo in Sparkwell and have changed their name again to The Wolf Centre and Dog Education.

They should be moving to a new place in Callington, Cornwall.

The Wolf Centre holds various courses on dogs as well as wolves / wolf hybrids – here are just a few –

***Wolf Introduction / Awareness Day** – this is where you will learn about the pack structure and also Visual, Vocal and Scent Communication.*

***Basic Wolf Course** – before you can do this course you should have completed the Wolf Awareness day. This is where you would learn about Field Work, Research Techniques, Survival and Tracking Skills. You would also learn about the Wolf Language and Behaviour that is used in Communications.*
The Course lasts two days.

***Intermediate Wolf Course** – before you can do this course you should have successfully completed the Basic Wolf Course. This is where you will learn more about the various types of Wolf Communication and their behaviour, this is a continuation from the Basic Course.*
On top of everything else you have learned, you will be taught Discipline, Husbandry, Diet and Feeding, Welfare and Hygiene, Basic Health, Methods of Recording Data, Equipment and Clothing, Food Preparation and Storage, Predator Awareness and Tracking to Locate.
Completion of this Course would allow acceptance onto the Volunteer Selection.
The Course lasts four days and two evenings.

***Advanced Wolf Course** – before you can do this course you should have successfully completed the Intermediate Wolf Course. This is where you will have a greater depth and expansion of all that you have learned in the Intermediate Course along with Survival and Tracking Scenarios.*
The Course lasts ten days.

Wolf Hybrid Encounter – *this is usually with the wolf hybrid in the enclosure but could be on the fence line, it lasts about an hour*

Shaun Ellis Experience – *this is the same as the Wolf Hybrid Encounter only it is with Shaun Ellis where you can ask him questions etc. again this lasts about an hour*

Extended Shaun Ellis Experience – *this lasts about one and a half hours and you also get to see some of the wolf packs*

Wolf Encounter – *where you will meet the wolves at the fence line and also behind the scenes, this lasts about an hour*

VIP Wolf Centre Experience – *this is where you will be given a tour of the centre and meet the wolves, spend lunch with Shaun Ellis and then have a meet and greet with the wolf hybrids. This lasts about three hours.*

The wolves at the Centre include –

Yana *the alpha male*

Tamaska *the enforcer a male wolf*

Matsi *the tester a male wolf*

Nanoose *a male wolf*

Cheyenne *their only pure bred female Timber wolf*

Tejas *the enforcer a smaller version of Tamaska*

Nataa *a male wolf decision maker*

Baby H *a female hybrid*

The wolf hybrids at the Centre include –

Wyakin *the male enforcer*

Hera *the female tester and* **Peaches** *another female hybrid*

*Other courses at the Centre are – **Dog Courses** of which include, Understanding your dog a one day and five day course then there is Understanding Aggression, Understanding Trauma, Understanding Socialisation, Understanding Separation Anxiety, Understanding Environment and Community and Understanding Feeding and Food Selection. Each of these courses lasts approximately two days.*
*They also have **Instructor Training** on Understanding your Dog which is comprised of five courses which can last up to twenty-eight days.*
*Finally **Dog and Puppy Schooling***

I am not sure if they are still doing individual Wolf Sponsorships or Pack Sponsorships you will have to check on their web site – details of which are in Chapter eight.

Another Wolf Society, which I have not visited as yet, but is worthy of a mention here is The Anglian Wolf Society based in North Bedfordshire.

It was founded in 1999 by Phil Watson with Co-Director Caroline Elliot and is a non-profit organisation. Their aim is to educate and inform the general public about wolves, support wolf conservation and to give people the chance to work with or study the wolves.
They acquired their first wolf pups in the spring of 2001 and they produce regular Newsletters consisting of Wolf Conservation, Behaviour, Book Reviews and updates on their own wolves.

They visit Country Shows / Fairs this is with or without their wolves

They have four socialised wolves which are –

Cheza a European wolf who is the alpha male

Peyto a Carpathian male wolf born on April 29th 2001

Kaya a North American x European female wolf born on April 22nd 2006 An attention seeker.

Alyana a North American x European female wolf born on April 22nd 2006 Alyana is Independent and a little shy. Both Kaya and Alyana are the siblings of Cheza

The Anglian Wolf Society have a range of Visits – here is just a selection –

Personal Observation Visit *– this is for the person who just wants to sit and watch the wolves in peace and quiet. Maybe take a picture or two*
This lasts about an hour

Wolf Experience Visit *– the wolves are usually fed during the visit giving you a unique photo opportunity. There are free refreshments and you receive a free Wolf Information Pack.*
*There is also a **Personal Wolf Experience Visit** – where you are the only person as opposed to a group.*

Wolf Walk Visit *– where there is a talk about the wolves and conservation work and the wolves are usually fed during the visit, [This is a good opportunity for photographs] plus free refreshments.*
You will also be on a walk with one of the wolves which can last from half an hour to one hour.

VIP Wolf Experience Visit *– this is a one on one private viewing of the wolves where you will meet and greet at the fence line. You will also get to feed the wolves and encourage them to howl.*
You will receive a free Wolf Information Pack, free refreshments and a Certificate of Achievement.
This lasts about three hours
You also have the opportunity to help clean out the pens while the wolves are in the holding area, this is optional.

Open Days *– these last about three hours and include Educational Games for the youngsters, Quizzes for the adults, a visit to the Owls, Llamas and Alpacas, lots of photo opportunities and a howl with the pack as well as meeting with the wolves.*

Adopt a Wolf *– when you adopt a wolf you will receive an A4 colour photo of your chosen wolf, an Adoption Certificate, a brief history plus character assessment of your chosen wolf and discounts on visits to the Society.*

Individual / Personal Photography

Wolf Experience and Llama Walk *– this starts around 10.00am with a talk on the wolves and Conservation Projects – you will receive free tea / coffee*

The wolves will be fed giving you unique photo opportunities, next would be lunch where free sandwiches are provided.
Around 12.30pm you will go on a Llama / Alpaca walk where two people share one Llama / Alpaca, this walk lasts about one hour.

Howl Nights

***Shadow the Keeper** – this starts around 10.00am with a welcome talk, you will meet and greet the wolves at the fence line, feed them and encourage them to howl. There will be lots of photo opportunities.*
You will help clean out the pens plus make food trails for enrichment feeding.
There is free tea / coffee available and at the end, around 2.30pm, you will receive a Certificate of Achievement.

Please note that all these events may change at any time and it would be best if you check their web sites for up to date information.

Web site addresses are listed in Chapter 8

Chapter 7

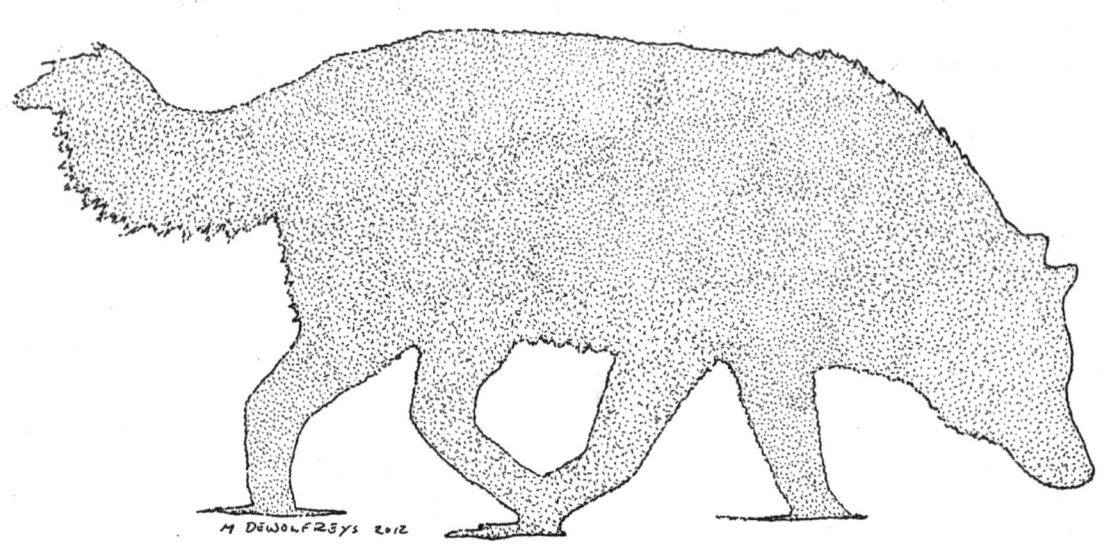

Wolf Reintroduction

As many of you will already know, there is talk of reintroducing wolves to Scotland, this should have taken place back in 2005 but so far this has been delayed.

The reintroduction is not as a result of action by the Wolf Fraternity but from people trying to regenerate the traditional forests and wildlife in Scotland. People were concerned at the declining numbers of Red Deer in Scotland so they put in place a programme to reverse the decline and at around the same time there were calls to reduce the amount of commercially grown alien trees and replace them with indigenous trees. Unfortunately the increased numbers of Red Deer ate the growing shoots of the new trees, this was a situation that the Forestry people could see being cured by the reintroduction of the Deer's natural predator, the wolf.

This is not likely to come about in the short or medium term but in the long term it is possible that reintroduction of the wolf would take place.

The first step would be Public Education, people, including professional conservationists, must be aware of the real wolf, that they are a part of our natural inheritance. People must know what happened to the wolves in the

Highlands, the benefits, drawbacks and potential impact they would have on the ecology and economy.

Secondly you need the agreement of the Government for a reintroduction, the Conservation Agency in Scotland is called the Scottish Natural Heritage, they are the body that would, largely, control the reintroduction. The Agency relies on the goodwill of Landowners and Farmers to further their conservation achievements. Landowners and Farmers are few in number but they control most of the land in Britain, around half the land in the Scottish Highlands is owned by approximately a hundred people, therefore, just a few people can be influential. And Scottish Natural Heritage does not want to upset them for the sake of a single species. Even the large conservation organisations will not support reintroduction if it upsets the Landowners, whilst the smaller organisations adopt a wait and see attitude, preferring to follow the larger organisations.

There would be no recovery if people are ignorant about wolves and there is plenty of food in the Highlands for them to exist.

The difference between reintroduction and recovery are as follows –

***Reintroduction** – this is the release of individuals that can take place in a single day, although this may not be successful as the subsequent recovery of the wolf population may fail. The individual wolves may all die out after a few years.*

***Recovery** – this is only successful when the population of released wolves increases in size and is unlikely to die out in the foreseeable future. Therefore a recovery is about a population and an ongoing process that could last years.*

There are some Treaties and Agreements that Britain should consider using the possibility of reintroducing the wolves under. These are the Bern Convention of the Council of Europe and Habitats Directive of the European Union.

I will try and explain which parts of each Treaties and Agreements are relevant to the reintroduction of wolves and what their aim is.

***Bern Convention** – the Convention on the conservation of European Wildlife and Natural Habitats was signed in Bern, Switzerland in 1979 and* *came into force in 1982, the aim is to conserve wild animals and plants along with their natural habitats, so far the Convention has signed over thirty European Nations from Portugal to Azerbaijan, including the United Kingdom.*

From time to time the committee makes additions to the Convention, these are called Recommendations.

One of these Recommendations is as follows –

***Recommendation Number 17** [1989] of the Standing Committee on the protection of the wolf, [canus lupus], in Europe.*

The parties to the Convention, including Britain, under Item A13 are required to consider the possibility of carrying out captive breeding and reintroduction programmes in areas where the species has been extinct or is endangered.

And under Item H are required, where the wolf has disappeared, to support actively the Conservation of this species. Particularly by promoting public awareness, encouraging research in its present distribution area, studying reintroduction possibilities and collaborating with the States where wolves survive.

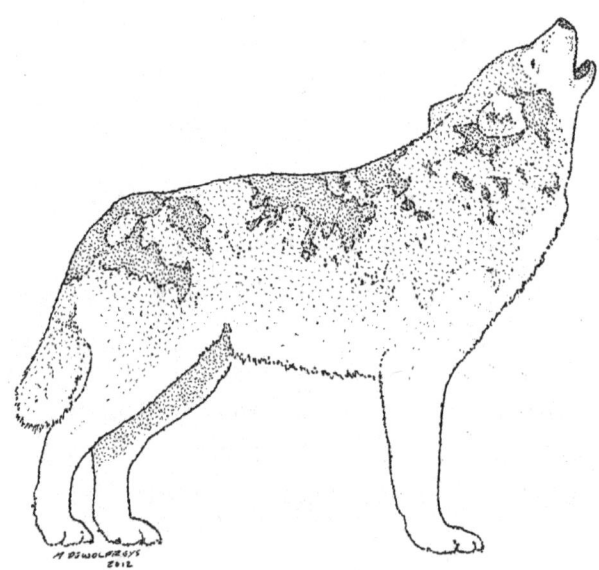

***Habitats Directive** – the European Unions Council Directive 92/43/EEC on the Conservation of Natural Habitats and Wild Fauna and Flora was adopted in Brussels, Belgium in 1992.*

The main aim of the Habitats Directive is to promote the maintenance of biodiversity. Article 22 reads – In implementing the provisions of this Directive, Member States shall –
[a] Study the desirability of reintroducing species in Annex IV that are native to their territory.

[The species in Annex IV are in need of strict protection and that includes the wolf]

The third step in the Highland reintroduction is an Environmental Impact Study, this is a guide on the practicalities of reintroducing wolves, essential for informed public debate and crucial for convincing the Secretary of State for Scotland, who must authorise a release of wolves, and a stipulation for the reintroduction by the World Conservation Union and by the Council of Europe.
The Environmental Impact Study research questions such as –

- *The suitability of the Highlands for wolves*

- *The attitude of the public towards a reintroduction*

- *The identification of potential wolf / human problems*

- *Whether a wolf recovery programme might succeed.*

Reintroducing the wolf to the Scottish Highlands is not a relatively new idea, it was first proposed in the late 1960s, then after the Red Wolf was reintroduced in the South Eastern United States in 1989 and the Grey Wolf reintroduced in Yellowstone National Park in 1995 the idea of the Scottish Highlands gained wider publicity and support.

A report published in 2007 entitled Wolf Reintroduction to Scotland : Public attitudes and consequences for Red Deer Management concluded that reintroduction of wolves to the Scottish Highlands would have significant ecological benefit by limiting numbers of Red Deer, reducing the need for costly Deer culls and allowing natural regeneration of the Caledonian Pine Forest.

One of the aspects of reintroduction of wolves into the Scottish Highlands would be Tourism.

Paul Lister who owns the Alladale Estate, North of Inverness, wants to bring back extinct native animals into the Scottish Highlands such as Wolves, Elk, Wild Boar and Brown Bears. They would be enclosed into a large fenced reserve similar to the game reserves in South Africa where tourists pay to view the animals.

If it proves successful this might persuade other landowners and businesses in Scotland to support the reintroduction.

At the moment this is a long way off.

Chapter 8

Epilogue, Wolf Quiz and References

I hope you enjoyed my little book, I have tried to be as authentic as possible with the available facts I have gathered together. However, as time progresses so too does new information, what was knowledgeable when I began to write this book is probably now superseded by new discoveries.
At the very least I hope I have managed to give a new insight into the world of wolves, and to show that they are not at all as aggressive as they have been portrayed in the movies, books and fairy tales.
Finally I must mention the pioneering and wonderful work that the Wolf Centre, The Anglian Wolf Society and the UKWolf Conservation Trust have done in educating the general public into the lives of wolves, without their help I believe many wolves would have been needlessly hunted and killed.
Of course there are many other Trusts and Centres around the world that also do a wonderful job in re-educating the general public that I have not mentioned in this book.
Anyway I hope you have been paying attention as I have a little wolf quiz for you to try, the answers are in Chapter 10

Wolf Quiz

Spot the Wolf

A   *B*   *C*

D   *E*   *F*

True or False

1   An adult wolf can sometimes have blue eyes

2   Wolves can swim a distance of up to eight miles [13k]

3   Wolves run on their toes

4   A wolf can hear up to four miles away in a forest and up to eight miles away in the Tundra.

5   Ireland was once called Wolf-land

6   Where there are wolves there are often ravens

7   The Japanese word for wolf means " Friend "

8   Wolves were the first animals to be placed on the US Endangered Species Act list in 1973

9   The wolf was the first animal to be domesticated by man

10 For a new wolf cub to urinate, its mother has to massage its belly with her warm tongue

Spot the wolf print

A   B   C

References

There are probably lots more reference books, DVD's and Web Sites that also offer unique information on wolves, I have only mentioned just a small sample below.

Books

The Ecology and Behaviour of an Endangered Species – L David Mech
ISBN 0816610266
University of Minnesota Press

The Wolf Talk – Shaun Ellis
ISBN 189905703-X
Rainbow Publishing

Spirit of the Wolf – Shaun Ellis and Monty Sloan
ISBN 140546321-X
Parragon Publishing

DVD

Lobo – The wolf that changed America
BBC Natural World

The Wolfman – Shaun Ellis
Aquavita Films

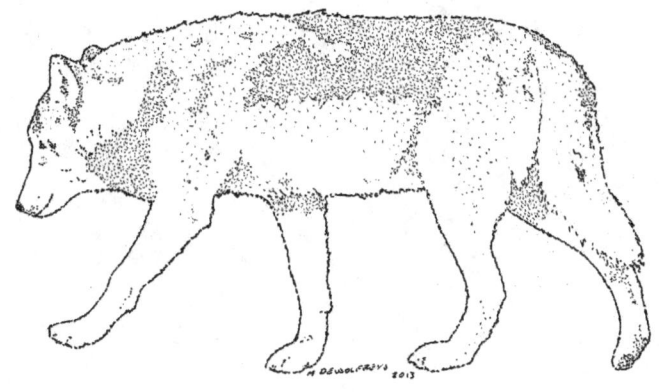

Web Sites

www.wwuk.org
Wolf Watch UK based near the Welsh border

www.ukwolf.org
UKWolf Conservation Trust based in Reading – see Chapter 6

www.thewolfcentreanddogeducationcentre.co.uk
Shaun Ellis – see Chapter 6

www.wolf.org
The International Wolf Centre based in Minnesota

www.dewolfguesthouse.com
Mark Dewolfreys web site based in Newquay Cornwall

www.wolvesandhumans.org
*Wolves and Humans Foundation established in 2005 it was originally called
The Wolf Society of Great Britain which was formed in 1985.*

www.anglianwolf.com
The Anglian Wolf Society based in Wootton

Chapter 9

Illustration and Photograph Listing

Chapter 10

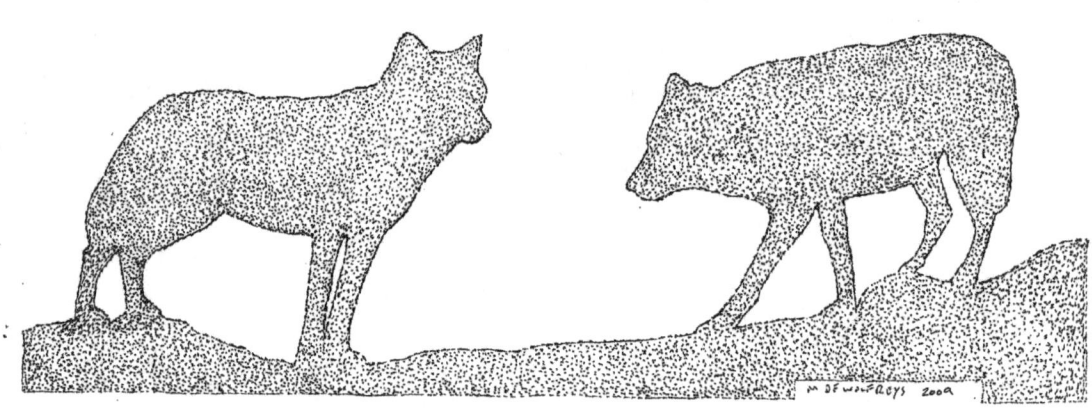

Finally, Quiz Answers and Further Facts

If you are thinking about a career in Wolf Husbandry or just want to know more about these fascinating creatures, I would fully recommend going on the various courses available from such places as The UKWolf Conservation Trust, The Anglian Wolf Society or The Wolf Centre and Dog Education Centre..

These are just a few places in the UK that offer various courses from the very basic to the more advanced. You could even help by volunteering your services or raise funds to help keep their organisations going; maybe you could sponsor one of their wolves.

I really do hope that one day the Governments from around the World will eradicate the practices of rewards being offered to hunters for wolf pelts, if they want to reduce wolf numbers in certain areas then they should use organised wolf culling carried out by official Government Organisations or even relocation programmes and not by profiteering hunters who can get up to £200 per pelt.

Wolf Quiz Answers

Spot the Wolf

If you answered B, D and E – you would be correct

True or False

1. *False – only wolf pups eyes are blue at birth but by the time they are around eight months old they turn yellow*

2. *True*

3. *True – as this helps them to stop and turn quickly it also helps to prevent their pads from wearing down*

4. *False – wolves can hear up to six miles away in a forest and up to ten miles away in the Tundra*

5. *True – back in the 1600s Ireland was called " Wolf-land " because they had so many wolves living there*

6. *True – Ravens or wolf-birds, often follow the wolves to grab leftovers from the hunt and also to tease the wolves whilst they eat.*

7. *False – the Japanese word for wolf means " Great God "*

8. *True*

9. *True – around 10,000 years ago*

10. *True*

Spot the Wolf Print

If you answered B you are correct, A - was a Panther and C – was a Dog

Further Facts

A 2008 study at Stanford University found that the mutation for black fur only occurs in dogs, so black coloured wolves are the result of Grey Wolves breeding with dogs. Black coloured wolves show an improvement in their immunity system to certain infections.
Black wolves are far more common in North America than the rest of the world.

The Vikings wore wolf skins and drank the blood of the wolf to take on its spirit in battle

Wolves were once the most widely distributed land predator the world had ever seen.

Tapetum Lucidum which is a layer of tissue in the eye, reflects light back inside – this assists the wolf in low light vision and, of course, causes the eyes to glow in the dark.

The first-century Greek Scholar, Pliny the Elder, believed that wolf teeth rubbed on the gums of infants eased the pain of teething and that wolf dung could be used for both Colic and Cataracts – I know – don't ask me how it was administered.

The Aztecs used a sharpened wolf bone to prick a person's breast in order to delay death. – I would think this would do the opposite

During the Middle Ages dried wolf meat was eaten as a remedy for sore shins

The Cherokee Indians would not hunt wolves as they believed that the wolf's brothers would exact revenge and that the weapon used would become useless

Well I really hope you liked my little book on wolves, and that you have learned a few facts you did not know before. I think the following Illustration shows you the learning curve that you go through when you study the animal at first hand rather than listening to the scaremongers.

It is entitled – Two faced – and it represents the wolf we know now and the wolf we were told about in fairy tales.

Please check out my other books – here are just a few

**Siberian Huskies
[a personal view]**
Mark Dewolfreys
ISBN : 978-1-4709-0792-1

*This is my personal standard description on the Siberian Husky from its early history to the present day.
Illustrated with my own drawings and photographs*

**Siberian Huskies
[a second view]**
Mark Dewolfreys
ISBN : 978-1-291 - 74597-9

*This is my own personal standard description of the Siberian Husky from their early history to the present day.
It is also an account of my own Siberian Huskies I rescued along the way
The book is lovingly Illustrated with my own Pen and Ink drawings as well as photographs taken over the years.*

From a woof to a howl
Mark Dewolfreys
ISBN : 978-1-4709-3630-3

This is my book on the various dogs that I have known or owned over the years, from my first canine companion to the present day.
Illustrated with my own pen and ink drawings and photographs taken over the years.

Close Encounters with the Misunderstood Wolf
Mark Dewolfreys
ISBN : 978-1-4478-6612-1

This is my personal standard description on wolves together with my wolf encounters I have had over the years.
Illustrated with my own drawings and photographs.

An Illustrated View of Huskies
Mark Dewolfreys
ISBN : 978-1-4709-3636-5

*This is my book of Illustrations
and photographs of my two
Siberian Huskies
Showing them laying, sleeping,
hunting, on alert and in various
poses*

***A Second Illustrated View of
Huskies***
Mark Dewolfreys
ISBN : 978-1-291-76281-5

*This is my book of over one
hundred and seventy-five
Illustrations and photographs
of my three
Siberian Huskies plus several
others were created
between 2010 - 2014
Showing them laying,
sleeping, hunting, on alert
and in various other poses.*

Thank you, my work here is done